Snooze-a-Palooza!

More Than 100 Slumber Party Ideas

Illustrated by
Carol Yoshizumi

★ American Girl™

Published by Pleasant Company Publications
Copyright © 2005 by American Girl, LLC

Questions or comments? Call 1-800-845-0005,
visit our Web site at **americangirl.com,** or write
American Girl, P.O. Box 620497, Middleton, WI 53562-0497.

Printed in China.
05 06 07 08 09 10 LEO 10 9 8 7 6 5 4 3

American Girl™ is a trademark of American Girl, LLC.

Editorial Development: Sara Hunt, Jessica Hastreiter

Art Direction: Camela Decaire, Chris Lorette David

Design: Camela Decaire

Production: Jeannette Bailey, Judith Lary, Kendra Schluter, Mindy Rappe

Illustrations: Carol Yoshizumi

Photography: Radlund Photography

Stylists: Camela Decaire, Lisa Wilber

Portions of this book previously appeared in *American Girl* magazine.

Cataloging-in-Publication Data is available from the Library of Congress.

Special thanks to Shelby H., Allie K., Kelsey H., Michelle H., Natalie H., Katie D., and Girl Scout Troop 257.

Dear American Girl,

Are you planning a sleepover soon? Looking for ideas to fill a whole night with your friends?

It's much easier to come up with ideas when you have a **theme.** A theme is like a recipe for planning a perfect party. And when everything ties together—from the invitations to the games, snacks, and activities, to the breakfast and favors—it makes for a more **memorable event.**

This book gives you a **step-by-step guide** to planning eight perfect sleepovers. You can stick to the **ideas** in each party description, or pick your favorite basic theme, then substitute games, activities, and snacks from the other pages that sound good to you. **It's your party!**

Your friends at American Girl

Contents

Invitation Station

The invitation is your first chance to build excitement about your party. Try to tie it to your theme to give guests a sneak peek at the fun in store. Be sure to cover the basics: your name, the party location, day and time, and pick-up time. Include your phone number for RSVPs and a date by which you'd like to hear back. If you'd like your guests to bring anything special, write that on the invitation, too.

Guest List

Sleepovers are for a few good friends to spend a l-o-o-o-ng night of fun together. That old rule of inviting the same number of guests as your age might work fine for regular parties, but consider cutting that number in half for an all-night party. Keep in mind that an odd number of guests will make for an even number during games and activities—including you!

It's also a good idea to try to invite girls who know each other. It can be awkward to sleep at someone's house with a gaggle of giggling girls you don't know. At the very least, try to be sure each guest knows one other guest.

Party Plan

The secret to a successful sleepover lies in the behind-the-scenes planning. Get started at least three weeks before your party. Once you've picked a theme, read over the directions for crafts, games, and foods, and run it all by your mom or dad. Use the shopping guide in the back of the book to be sure you have everything you need.

Party Time

To help keep the fun on track, make a list of everything you plan to do at the party and when you hope to do it. At the party, though, be flexible. Something you thought would take 15 minutes might take only 2 minutes. Or your friends might like a game so much that they don't want to stop playing after the allotted time. It's better to overplan and to draw a star next to any activity that you consider to be optional.

LIST

- make Sock monkeys
- Serve food
- play monkey in the middle
- play monkey suit game
- watch movie

Game Faces

Games can make or break your party. You need them to keep the good times rolling, but some games can cause trouble among friends. Avoid games in which there's a clear winner or a definite loser. And, if someone doesn't want to play a particular game, don't make a big deal about it. Let her take a break and join in when she's ready.

Parent Patrol

Talk to Mom and Dad before the party so that you know what the ground rules are for your gang, and your parents know what you expect from them. Do you want a parent to hang around to help keep things rolling? Want Mom to step in if an argument crops up? Or would you rather run the show as much as possible? Same goes for siblings. To avoid a big fight, talk to your whole family in advance about your party.

Food Fun

Don't go overboard with menu ideas. Pick a few fun snacks or treats that tie to your theme—and that taste yummy! When you can, make food ahead of time.

If you (or your parents) want to avoid the dinner hour, start your party at 7:00 or 8:00 P.M. This also makes for a shorter evening to fill with activities. (Because you will probably be up very late!)

Several recipes in this book call for melted chocolate. Follow the instructions below to melt chocolate.

Melting Chocolate

In a microwave-safe measuring cup or small bowl, melt 3 white or milk chocolate baking bars (6 ounces), broken into pieces, on 70% power for 1 minute. Stir. If needed, microwave for 10 to 15 seconds at a time, stirring until smooth. Cool slightly. You may add 1 tablespoon vegetable shortening when melting chocolate to help it set.

Safety Note

Anytime you see this hand or when you think a project or recipe is too hard to do yourself, ask an adult to help you. Be sure an adult supervises any cutting or cooking. Also make sure you keep small pieces like beads, buttons, and dried beans put away so younger siblings don't eat them!

Sack Spots

As soon as your guests arrive, have them set up their sleeping bags in a separate room. Stock the area with books, magazines, and board games in case someone wants to turn in early and needs a little something quiet to do. Make sure guests know where the bathroom is, and leave a light on in the hall so that girls can find their way in the dark if they need to.

Sweet Dreams

Not everyone will think it's dreamy to tell scary stories at bedtime. For a funny twist, suggest that each girl tell a joke or funny story she knows instead.

Spa Night!

Pamper your pals from head to toe!

Invitation

Cut slipper shapes from construction paper. Glue together. Add some style with snips of marabou, a fuzzy pipe cleaner, or a pom-pom to decorate the top. Write party details on the sole of each slipper. Ask guests to bring their favorite CDs to play as you pamper yourselves.

It's Spa Night

at: Shayna's house
day: March 22
time: 5 p.m.
R.S.V.P. 555-4506

bring PJ's, slippers, and your favorite CD!

Spa Berries

Wash and dry strawberries, then dip them halfway into melted white or milk chocolate. Place on a wax paper-lined cookie sheet and refrigerate until set.

Powder Puffs

Have an adult help bake frozen puff pastry shells according to package instructions. Cool. Fill with whipped topping and sift powdered sugar on them. If you really want to indulge your guests, drizzle puffs with melted chocolate.

Beverages

Fill a large bowl with ice and bottles of "healthy" drinks.

Cool Cucumbers

Your spa party won't be complete without cucumber slices to help soothe those tired eyes. Here's a yummy idea for using any extra cuke slices:

Mix one 8-ounce package cream cheese, one package dry ranch dressing mix, and ½ cup sour cream in a small bowl. Split and toast mini bagels, and top with mixture. Add a cucumber slice and sprinkle with fresh dill (if you like it).

Head-to-Toe Treatment

NOTE: Have each girl test an area on the inside of her wrist first to see if any ingredients irritate her skin.

Face

Before the Party

Mash 3 bananas with 1½ tablespoons honey. Make sure you don't have any large chunks of banana. Store in the refrigerator until spa time.

Have a basket of ponytail holders or wide headbands so that guests can pull their hair up off their faces. Also, keep a stack of small clean towels near the sink.

Exfoliate

Pour a small amount of cornmeal into your hand, mix with warm water, and gently rub onto your face. Rinse with warm water and pat dry with a clean towel.

Refresh

Pamper your face with a banana-mash mask. Rub mask all over your face, avoiding areas around eyes, nostrils, and mouth. Lie down on your sleeping bag for about 15 minutes. Add two cucumber slices to rest those tired eyes. Rinse face with warm water.

YOGA
GIRL

Hands

Scrub

Pour a small amount of white sugar into the palm of one hand, mix with baby oil, then rub mixture all over your hands. Rinse hands with warm water and dry with a clean towel.

Soak

Remove nail polish. Soak fingertips in a bowl with 1 cup warm milk plus 1 tablespoon lemon juice for 5 to 10 minutes. Rinse off and dry.

Massage

Dab olive oil into cuticle area. Rub in.

Paint

Have an assortment of nail polish available to paint nails.

American Curls

Put everyone's name in a hat and draw a name to see who your stylist will be!

1 Cut an old T-shirt or pillowcase to make several 1-inch-wide strips about 2 inches longer than your hair. Use a spray bottle to lightly mist hair.

2 Pick up a small section of hair. Hold one end of a fabric strip close to the head and run it alongside the hair section. Wrap hair around the strip, then bring up the other end and tie at the scalp. Sleep on the curls, then in the morning, untie for a headful of soft curls.

Beauty Secrets

Gather pairs of spa items to play a fun matching game. (See list for ideas.)

Before the party, place a variety of the items in paper sacks for each girl (making sure that everyone has the same number of items and that no one has both items from any pair). The more items you have, the trickier the game is to play.

Players take turns asking each other if they have an item to match something in their bags. For example, Emma might ask, "Allie, do you have a nail polish?" If Allie does, she gives it to Emma and Emma earns a "match." The first player to match all of her items is the winner!

2 cotton balls
2 cotton swabs
2 washcloths
2 ponytail holders
2 mini soaps
2 tubes lip gloss
2 toothbrushes
2 nailbrushes
2 mini shampoos
2 mini lotions
2 nail clippers
2 nail polishes
2 hairbrushes
2 combs
2 hair clips

Truth . . . or Not?

Give each girl paper and a pencil. Choose one girl to be It. It begins by stating something about herself, such as "I wear the same pair of socks every Monday." Each girl writes down whether she thinks the statement is true or false. Then It reveals her answer. Give one point for each correct guess. If no one guessed correctly, It gets a point. The girl with the most points at the end gets to choose the next CD.

Power Memory

Bring out a basketful of spa supplies and have everyone look at them for 30 seconds. Remove the basket and ask guests to write down as many items as they can remember. Bring the basket back and list the items. The person who remembered the most gets to choose an item from the basket as a prize.

Relaxation Station

Give each girl a handheld massage roller. Have guests sit in a row or circle, and each girl gently roll-massages the back and shoulders of the girl in front of her. Have guests turn around and repeat, if desired.

Lotion Sampler

Supply a variety of types and fragrances of body lotion for guests to try on their arms, legs, hands, and feet.

Paste Test

Before calling it a night, try a fun-flavored toothpaste like cinnamon, berry, or citrus.

Smart Start

Start your day with fruit smoothies. Then play a yoga tape as girls wait to be picked up.

To make smoothies, put ½ cup frozen fruit (try strawberries, blueberries, or bananas), ⅓ cup orange juice, 1 single serving container yogurt, and 4 or 5 ice cubes in a blender. Cover and ask an adult to blend until smooth. Serves 2.

Pamper Packs

Let guests take their special treatment on the road with a travel-sized shampoo and lotion, a cute nail clipper, a comb, and a brush all rolled or tied with a ribbon into a pretty washcloth.

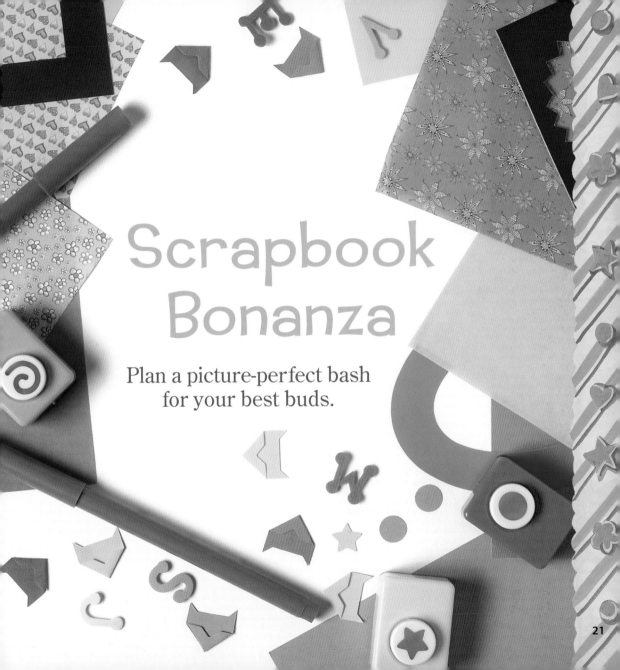

Scrapbook Bonanza

Plan a picture-perfect bash
for your best buds.

Invitation

Make invitations from envelopes, stickers, and scrapbook supplies. Ask guests to use the envelopes to bring photos to the party.

Let's get Scrappy!

TOP SECRET

Bring your favorite baby photo!

Bring your favorite photos and come spend the night at Katelyn's Scrapbook Bonanza

CUTIE

Hey, Baby!

Ask guests to bring baby pictures of themselves along with their photos for their scrapbooks. Lay the baby pictures on a table and place a number next to each one. Give each girl a piece of paper and a pencil and have her write down who's who. See who gets the most correct guesses.

Paper Punch Confetti

Decorate the party table with scraps from punched scrapbook paper. Use a variety of punches to make little circles, stars, and hearts. Pick a theme to match the season or reason for your party!

Photo Cake

Ask if your local bakery can print a scanned color photo onto the top of a cake. If so, instead of a photo, provide a color copy of a favorite scrapbook page (one that might include photos of all the guests).

Make photo corners from snips of Fruit Roll-Ups. Decorate the edges of the cake with confetti candy sprinkles.

Stock Up

Provide each girl with a mini scrap-book. Then stock up on scrapbook paper, stickers, specialty scissors, and tons of paper punches.

Add some of your own doodles and notes to tell the story.

Use photo frames or create your own frames from patterned paper.

Use die cuts or paper-punch shapes for added interest.

Give each page a theme. Create letters or use alphabet stickers for a title.

Make shapes from paper.

Try cutting photos into more interesting shapes.

Cut someone out of a photo and draw a scene around her.

Table Talkers

Write a few conversation starters on scrap paper and put them in a small box or bag in the center of the table. Here are a few, for starters:

- If you could go anywhere in the world, where would you go?
- If you could choose a nickname for yourself, what would it be?
- If you won a million dollars, what would you do with it?
- What was the best present you ever got?

Have each girl add a question to the bag. Then pull one out anytime you want to get the chatter flowing!

Scrap Bookmark

Use leftover scraps of scrapbook paper and stickers to make yourself a personalized scrap bookmark! Cover it with clear contact paper to make it more durable. Punch a hole in the top and tie with a colorful ribbon.

Studio Time

Set up a photo booth in a corner. Ask an adult to hang a colorful shower curtain or sheet as a backdrop. Have guests stand in front of the backdrop while you take instant pictures. Supply props such as silly hats or sunglasses for extra-goofy shots.

Rotating Page

Cut several pieces of scrapbook paper the same size as a page in the scrapbooks. Pass out one page to each girl. She attaches her photo (from the Studio), then passes her page to the person on her left. Each girl decorates part of the page and writes nice things about that girl. After a few minutes, everyone passes her page again. Continue passing the pages around until each girl has her own page back. Each guest can use her page for the first page of her mini scrapbook.

Say "Cheese!"

It might seem kind of "cheesy," but you can get everyone smiling at your party with an all-cheese menu. Start things off with munchies like cheese puffs, cheese popcorn, or cheddar-flavored crackers. Later, serve your favorite cheesy dinner—cheese pizza, mac 'n' cheese, grilled-cheese sandwiches, or cheeseburgers.

Confetti Cookies

These are perfect for munching all through the night. Pour candy sequins onto a paper plate. Spread frosting onto colorful vanilla wafer cookies. Dip cookies into sprinkles, then fill a platter with these colorful treats.

Confetti Eggs

Add diced red, yellow, and green bell peppers to your scramblers in the morning. Sprinkle eggs with shredded cheddar or Monterey Jack cheese.

Scrap Bags

Send your friends home with extra stickers and scrapbook paper to help them finish their memory books. Add an assortment of supplies, such as paper punches, rubber stamps and ink pads, some gel or specialty pens, photo corners, or paper die cuts. Put all the supplies in expandable plastic folders. You can even give out disposable cameras, so your friends will keep snapping AND scrapping!

Monkey Business

Get the gang together—and go bananas!

Invitation

Use paper and craft-foam shapes to make invitations. Craft cute chimps from two sizes of ovals and a circle. The mouth is an oval cut lengthwise, and ears are oval halves. Attach with craft glue. Add google eyes.

Use a paper fastener to attach your party details. Your card will swing open!

Swing by...

If a local gym offers "open gym" hours, take the group to monkey around.

Funky Monkey Milk Shakes

Put 2 scoops chocolate ice cream into a blender. Pour in ½ cup milk. Add 1 large peanut butter cup and ½ banana. Cover and ask an adult to blend on HIGH until smooth. Pour into glasses. Top with whipped cream, if desired. Sprinkle with crushed peanut butter cups. Makes 2 large or 4 small milk shakes. For decoration, hang a plastic monkey on each glass.

Monkey Tails

Be sure to serve up some of these cool snacks! Peel bananas and cut them in half. Insert a wooden stick into each cut end. Place bananas on wax paper on a cookie sheet. Put in freezer for 2 hours. Right before the 2 hours is up, fill separate bowls with toppings, such as chopped peanuts or colored sprinkles. Roll frozen bananas in chocolate sauce. Sprinkle on toppings. Return bananas to freezer until ready to serve.

Monkey See, Monkey Do

Players take turns being the Monkey. The Monkey secretly picks a special "move" (for example, she rests her chin on her hand), and then sometime during the party, she does it. The last person to do what the Monkey did is the new Monkey.

Sock Monkeys

While you're hanging around, make monkey buddies from socks and beans!

YOU WILL NEED

- **Red-Heel socks**
- **Rubber bands**
- **Dried beans**
- **Craft glue**
- **Buttons**

1 Turn the sock inside out. Use a rubber band to close off the toe about 1 inch below the heel. Turn sock right-side out. Fill about 4 inches with small dried beans.

2 Close off the rest of the sock with a rubber band. The heel of the sock should be the monkey's muzzle.

3 Pinch a section on either side of the sock to make ears. Secure each ear with a rubber band. Glue on button eyes.

4 Fold the top of the sock over to make a hat.

Get Out of That Monkey Suit!

Fill 2 suitcases, each with a complete work outfit from your mom's or dad's closet (with their permission, of course!). Don't forget accessories like clip-on earrings, a tie or scarf, belt, socks, shoes, even panty hose and a slip! There should be an equal number of items in each suitcase.

Divide your guests into 2 equal teams. On "go," players take turns running with the suitcase to a designated spot across the room, putting on every item in the suitcase over their regular clothes, and running back to the group. The next person in line helps the previous player "get out of her monkey suit," repacks the suitcase, runs across to the dressing spot, and repeats the process. The first team to get all players in and out of their monkey suit wins.

Monkey in the Middle

Girls pair up and link arms with a partner. Pairs form a large circle. Two girls do not pair up—one is the Monkey in the Middle, and the other is It. On "go," It tries to tag the Monkey. To be safe, the Monkey picks a girl to link arms with before getting tagged. Now the other girl from that pair becomes It, and the previous It becomes the Monkey in the Middle. You might need lots of space to play this fun one!

Cupcake Faces

Mix equal parts of white and chocolate frosting to make light brown. Frost cupcakes, adding mini peanut butter sandwich cookie ears. Use mini M&M's for eyes. Center a mini vanilla wafer on each cupcake for a muzzle. Put a smile or a smirk on each face with a snip of red licorice rope secured with a dab of icing.

Watch *MVP: Most Valuable Primate* (or one of the sequels!), or *Summer of the Monkeys*.

Favors

Your friends will go bananas over goody bags stuffed with things such as monkey-print socks, headbands, bookmarks, earrings, coin purses, door hangers, or pens.

Monkey Muffins

Rouse sleepyheads with the delicious smell of monkey muffins in the oven!

1 Grease tins for 24 muffins. Sprinkle ½ cup chopped pecans evenly in bottom of muffin cups.

2 Mix 1 teaspoon cinnamon and ½ cup sugar in a large ziplock bag. Separate biscuits from four 7½-ounce cans of refrigerated buttermilk biscuits, and break apart each biscuit into three pieces.

3 Shake several biscuit pieces in the cinnamon mixture. Place 5 pieces in each muffin cup.

4  Have an adult melt 1 stick of butter in a microwave-safe bowl. Add 1 cup firmly packed brown sugar. Spoon mixture over muffins.

5 Have an adult bake muffins at 350 degrees for 15 minutes. Cool 10 minutes in the pan. Use a spoon to scoop out each muffin onto a serving plate. Remove any topping bits that fall off. Serve warm.

cocoa
loco

Treat your friends to a celebration that's as sweet as they are!

Invitation with Taste!

Carefully remove the outer wrapper from a chocolate bar. Trace around the outside of the wrapper onto the back of a piece of scrapbook paper. Cut out, then write party details on the back side. Rewrap the chocolate bar and tape closed. Decorate the outside with stickers and the guest's name.

CHOCOLATE PARTY!
Saturday
October 1
Paige's House
R.S.V.P.
5-6274

SARAH

Hot Chocolate
Late
cool
hat

What's in Hot Chocolate?

Pass out paper and pencils and ask everyone to write as many words as she can find in HOT CHOCOLATE. Give each girl a Hug or Kiss (chocolate, of course!) for each word she finds.

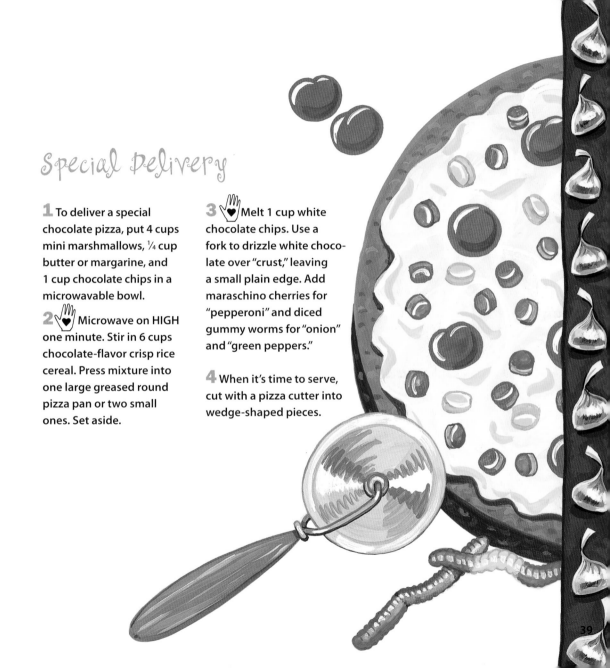

Special Delivery

1 To deliver a special chocolate pizza, put 4 cups mini marshmallows, ¼ cup butter or margarine, and 1 cup chocolate chips in a microwavable bowl.

2 Microwave on HIGH one minute. Stir in 6 cups chocolate-flavor crisp rice cereal. Press mixture into one large greased round pizza pan or two small ones. Set aside.

3 Melt 1 cup white chocolate chips. Use a fork to drizzle white chocolate over "crust," leaving a small plain edge. Add maraschino cherries for "pepperoni" and diced gummy worms for "onion" and "green peppers."

4 When it's time to serve, cut with a pizza cutter into wedge-shaped pieces.

The Chocolate Game

Play this fun game from Germany. Before the party, wrap a chocolate bar several times in gift wrap. (For an extra challenge, tie ribbon in a bow around the package.) Everyone sits in a circle. Give each girl a small paper plate. Put the wrapped chocolate bar in the middle, along with a scarf, a hat, a pair of gloves, and a table knife and fork. Players take turns rolling 2 dice. When a player's roll totals 6, she puts on the hat, scarf, and gloves and uses the knife and fork to rip open the package. If she breaks off a small piece of chocolate, she must pick it up with the knife and fork and put it on her plate (no eating!). She does as much as she can until someone else rolls a 6 and gets a turn.

Make S'more Nachos

Fold flour tortillas into quarters. Unfold and tear along the fold lines. Place several tortilla quarters onto a cookie sheet, then lightly spray both sides of each piece with cooking spray. Spread tortilla pieces with creamy peanut butter. Top with mini marshmallows and mini chocolate chips. Have an adult bake nachos at 475 degrees for 3 to 4 minutes until marshmallows are golden. You'll definitely want s'more!

Oopsa-loompahs

While your guests are taking in the gooey fun, run the video *Willy Wonka and the Chocolate Factory*. Watch for these and other movie mishaps:

- Look for at least 4 instances of "bad hair" that suddenly corrects itself in the next shot.

- Charlie watches TV to hear about the golden ticket, but when he turns around to talk to Grandpa, the TV is off.

- Look as Charlie is lifted in the Fizzy Lifting Drinks room—you can see there's a harness that lifts him up!

Um, Uh

Pick one person and give her a topic—for example, chocolate. That person has to talk about that subject for 30 seconds without saying "um" or "uh" or pausing for more than a few seconds.

Chocolate is derived from the cocoa bean. It comes in many different varieties, like dark, semisweet, and milk chocolate. Chocolate is a wonderful, sweet, melty treat and is great in cookies, cakes, hot cocoa,...

Terrific Truffles

Make chocolates with your chums. Before the party, ask an adult to prepare the truffle mixture: Put 3 cups semisweet chocolate chips and 1 can (14 ounces) sweetened condensed milk into a saucepan. Stir constantly over medium heat until chocolate is melted. Remove from heat and pour into a small bowl. Let cool for 2 hours.

Have your guests wash their hands. Let each girl roll some of the chocolate mixture into small balls, then dip the balls in candy decorations. Place each truffle in a paper candy cup (available at craft stores). Put truffles in small boxes (found at craft stores) for each girl to take home.

Candy Bar Smarts

Copy this page on a color copier and have each guest
guess what kind of candy bar is shown in each picture.
Answers are on the next page.

Chocolate Chippers

Have an adult add 1 cup chocolate chips, ½ teaspoon vanilla, and 1 tablespoon sugar to your favorite pancake-batter recipe. Top plate-sized pancakes with dollops of whipped cream and maraschino cherries. Wash them down with—what else?—chocolate milk!

Flavor-ite Favors

After eating chocolate all night, your friends will be happy to go home in the morning with goody bags full of nonedible chocolate treats, such as chocolate-scented soap, stickers, lotion, or markers, chocolate-themed hairbows, magnets, or earrings, and chocolate lip gloss.

44

Brrrr-day Party

Chill out with lots of totally cool things to do.

Invitation

Write the party details on a piece of paper. Cut a slightly larger piece of fleece or felt. Roll up the paper inside the fleece and tie with two strings.

Ice Breaker

You need up to 3 stuffed animals to play this fast-paced game. Ask girls to pick their favorite flavor of breakfast cereal. Go around the circle and have each player say her pick. To start, one player takes a stuffed animal and tosses it to another player. As she tosses, she says the name of that girl's favorite cereal. That girl catches the stuffed animal and tosses to someone else, saying her favorite. Keep trying to pick up the pace. Once everyone has the hang of it, add another animal so that two girls are tossing and catching at once. Try adding a third animal. Phew!

S'mittens

Decorate regular knit mittens or gloves with ribbon trims or fake fur attached with fabric glue. You'll need enough trim to go around each cuff, plus a few extra inches. As you work around the cuff, stretch the glove just a bit so that the cuff remains elastic. Once you've glued all the way around, cut the trim, leaving an extra ½ inch. Fold under the cut end and glue it down. Let dry.

Snowballs

Make 18 peanut butter and cracker sandwiches. Set aside. Melt 1 cup white chocolate in microwavable bowl. Dip cracker sandwiches into melted white chocolate. Place snowballs onto wax paper. Dot each snowball with 2 M&M's in cool colors. Let set.

Cool Scarf

You and your friends can stay warm and be cool at the same time by making snuggly fleece boas in your favorite colors.

1 Cut 6-by-40-inch strips of fleece. Cut enough so each girl has 2 pieces, one of each color. Squeeze a line of fabric glue lengthwise down the center of one fabric piece. Place other piece on top. Let dry.

2 Cut 1-inch-wide strips along the length of the fabric, being careful not to cut through the center glue line. Repeat on other side. Fluff and wear!

Chilly Cheese Dip

Have an adult melt 1 pound processed cheese with 1 can chili (no beans) in a microwave for 2 minutes. Stir. Serve with tortilla chips.

Hot & Zesties

Have an adult heat mini smoked sausages with your favorite bottled barbecue sauce. Serve with toothpicks or skewers.

Cold Feet

To wind down, bring out a few bottles of icy-colored nail polish such as cool blue or frosty white. Use fluffy cotton balls between toes for a mess-free pedicure!

Wintry Flick Picks

Watch a movie while you do your nails!

Ice Age
Snow Dogs
Snow Day
Johnny Tsunami

Stir It Up!

Melt several different kinds of baking chips in small microwavable bowls. Fill several more small bowls with a variety of stir-ins.

Dip plastic spoons into melted chips. Set on wax paper or aluminum foil. Sprinkle with your favorite treat to make your hot cocoa extra sweet! Let cool.

Try these dippers:

- Milk chocolate chips
- Butterscotch chips
- White chocolate chips
- Peanut butter chips
- Semisweet chocolate chips

Try swirling or drizzling two flavors.

Try these toppers:

- Crushed cookies
- Mini marshmallows
- Candy sprinkles
- Mini chocolate chips
- Crushed candies
- Mini M&M's

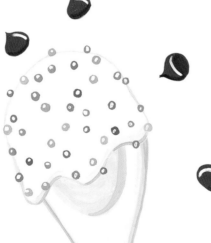

Use decorated spoons to stir hot chocolate, or wrap each spoon in a cellophane bag and tie with a ribbon to send home with your guests.

Morning Frost

No one will mind waking up to this morning frost—a plate piled high with powdered-sugar doughnuts. Serve juice in frosty mugs. *Brrrr!*

Cool Stuff

Stuff a wintry mug with minty gum, gift certificates for ice cream, frosty lip gloss or nail polish, and a hot-cocoa packet.

Board Silly

Gather up your games, then invite friends over
to play the night away.

Check-er Out This Invitation

Get the games going with tiny checkerboard invitations. For each guest, cut out a 2-inch-square piece of checkered paper. Write party details on a 1½-inch-square piece of white paper. Glue white paper in the middle of checkerboard. Fold in half. Cut red paper to fit around a matchbox. Write a guest's name with a white gel pen. Use a hole punch to cut out checkers from red and black craft-foam sheets. Tuck these inside the matchbox along with the invitation.

Tic-Snack-Toe

Use decorator icing to draw tic-tac-toe boards on frosted cupcakes. At the party, pass out M&M's. Each pair of players chooses a different color of candy and plays tic-tac-toe on a cupcake. The winner takes the cake!

You Don't Say!

Pick five words that no one is allowed to say during the party. Choose words such as "cake," "game," or other common ones. When guests arrive, give each one $500 in funny money. If you catch someone using one of the forbidden words, you get $100 of her funny money. The richest person at the end of the party wins!

Dice Cream

You can make these icy dice ahead of time, then put them in an air-tight container in the freezer until ready to use. Remove the carton from a half-gallon box of vanilla ice cream. Working quickly, dip a knife into warm water and ask an adult to help you slice ice cream into 2 cubes. Press mini chocolate sandwich cookies into top and sides of each cube to make delicious dice.

Games on the Go

Give each guest an empty metal candy tin. Paint the top of the lid with acrylic paint. Let dry about 45 minutes. Paint on a tic-tac-toe board. Let dry 30 minutes more. Press tiny stickers onto a magnetic sheet. Cut the stickers into squares that will fit in your board spaces. Carry the magnets in the tin for a quick game anytime.

Fuzzy Dice

Roll on into the night with this retro craft. Glue squares of fake fur onto small wooden cubes. Several colors of fur make the dice extra fun. Glue on colorful rhinestones to make the spots. Let dry.

Speed Games

Keep players perked up with a board game relay. Set up different game stations around the room to have enough spots for two guests at each station. Use games in which you can quickly tell who is ahead at any point. Set a timer for ten minutes. Play games until the time runs out. Determine the winner of each game and give her a point. Have guests trade partners and play again. Whoever has the most points at the end of four or five rounds is the speed games winner!

58

Giant Goofball Game

Just when guests start to wind down, turn up the fun with this goofy game. Give each guest three sheets of colored paper and a marker. Ask guests to write a quick activity on each colored sheet and directions for moving forward or backward. For example, you could say, "Tell a knock-knock joke and move ahead 3 spaces." When everyone is done, make a giant game board by laying out the colored papers in a path on the floor, placing 2 to 5 white sheets of paper between the colored ones.

To make a die, cover a large square box with paper. Draw on dots with a black marker. Roll the die, move ahead that many spaces, and follow the instructions on the paper where you land. If you land on a blank, stay there. The first player to finish is the winner!

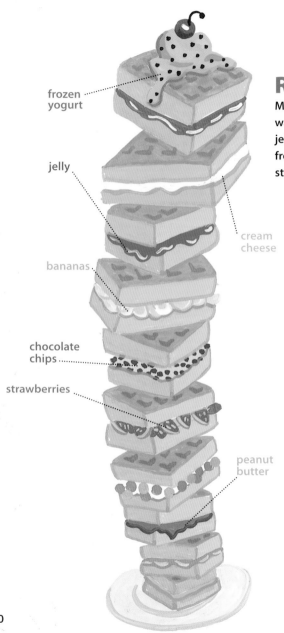

frozen
yogurt

jelly

cream
cheese

bananas

chocolate
chips

strawberries

peanut
butter

Rise and Dine!

Make waffle sandwiches! Toast frozen waffles and serve with peanut butter, jelly, cream cheese, chocolate chips, frozen yogurt, or fruit such as sliced strawberries or bananas.

Key Chain Keepsakes

Look for key chain games at toy, discount, or department stores. Give guests these fun favors, and everyone will be a winner!

BEADAZZLED BIRTHDAY

This bead-filled party's just the thing
to help you plan your next fling.

61

INVITATION

Here's a fun, delicious way to invite your guests! Write the party details on metal-rimmed key tags. Tie the tags to candy bracelets, and deliver!

Bead Party
7pm
June 17
Erin's House

CHILL OUT

Scoop out several flavors of ice cream to make this chilly treat extra sweet! Before the party, use a melon baller to scoop small balls of ice cream into a bowl. Dip the melon baller into warm water between scoops. Cover the bowl with plastic wrap and store in the freezer until party time.

TWIRL THE GIRL

Fill a bowl with different-colored beads. Make a list of the possible colors and pick an "answer" for each one, like this:

Green = Yes

Red = No

Pink = Maybe so

Purple = Definitely!

Tiger's Eye = Not a chance

Light Blue = Wait and see

To play, sit in a circle with one girl standing in the middle. Have each sitting girl pick a colored bead from the bowl. The girl in the middle twirls around with her eyes closed. When she stops, she asks a question, such as "Will I get a puppy for my birthday?" She opens her eyes. The girl sitting directly in front of her holds up the bead and gives the answer. That girl then moves to the center, and the game starts over. Pick new beads each time. Good luck!

BEAD-HAPPY BRACELETS

Make these beautiful bead-and-ribbon bracelets for party keepsakes.

YOU WILL NEED

- Wide embroidered ribbon
- Scissors
- Fabric glue
- Ruler
- 24-gauge craft wire
- Fingernail clippers
- Seed beads
- Buttons with shank (a loop on the back)

1 Cut ribbon to fit around wrist with no overlap. Fold each end of ribbon under ¼ inch. Glue in place.

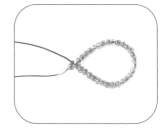

2 Cut a 2-foot piece of wire with fingernail clippers. Thread enough beads onto the center of the wire so that the button slips through when you form a loop. Thread one end of wire back through the last bead to make a loop.

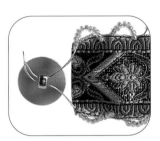

3 Thread 5 beads onto one side of wire. You will now work on this side only. Using the end of the wire like a needle, poke it through one side of the ribbon, close to the edge. Go through both layers of the folded-over end. Pull the wire snug.

4 Thread 10 beads onto the wire. Take another stitch from the same direction as the first, about ¼ inch away. Pull snug. Repeat until you get to the other end of the ribbon. Repeat steps 3 and 4 with the other wire on the opposite side of the ribbon.

5 Thread 5 beads onto each wire. Hold wires together and thread ends through button shank. Loop wires around shank and twist several times at base. Clip off any excess wire with fingernail clippers.

BEAD IT

If time runs short, fill small plastic bags with extra seed beads and a button so that guests can finish their bracelets later.

POWER COOKIES

Some people think that if you wear beads that are a certain color, they will give you lucky powers. Guests will find their own power-bead fortunes inside these chocolate-dipped cookies!

Cookies: For 8 fortune cookies, melt ½ cup chocolate chips. Dip half of each cookie in melted chocolate, then add candy sprinkles. Place cookies on wax paper until set.

Fortunes: Use the bead list below, or make up your own, and write wishes for good fortune on strips of paper. Punch a hole at one end of each paper. Tie on a power bead with matching thread. Stick paper into plain side of cookie.

POWER BEADS

 Turquoise: Health

 Mother-of-Pearl: Money

 Green: Success

 Black: Self-control

 Pink: Romance

 Purple: Truth

 Tiger's Eye: Creativity

 Crystal: Strength

 Red: Love

 Light Blue: Peace

SPEED BEAD

This fast and funny game is harder than it sounds! Give each player a different color of bead. Sit in a circle. To start, someone calls out a color. The player with that color bead immediately calls out another color (no pausing and no calling your own color), and so on. When a player goofs up, everyone passes her bead to the right and gets a new color. See how fast you can go!

BEADS & CHARMS

Mix up bowls of berry yummy "beads"—
melon balls, grapes, and blueberries.
Add colorful cereal for crunch. Make
bowls from scooped-out melon halves,
and top each off with a dollop of yogurt.

FAVOR FUN

Give guests power-bead favors that
match their wishes for good fortune!
Fill small plastic bags with beads and
a piece of elastic cord about 10 inches
long. Tie the bags shut with ribbon.

Truth

Success

Glitter Gala

This shindig simply sparkles from start to finish.

Invitation

Use markers to write party details on a crepe-paper streamer. Put scrap paper underneath while you write in case the ink bleeds through.

Leave extra space at the end so writing doesn't show. Roll up the streamer. Twist a length of star garland around it for a dazzling presentation.

You're Invited...
Kelsey's Glitter Gala
4 p.m. * May 9 * Kelsey's house * 555-0193

Wear Something Sparkly!

You Glow, Girl!

Here are a few ideas to add some glitter to your gala:

Greet your friends with a sprinkling of body glitter as they arrive.

Wrap metallic star garland or pipe cleaners around your ponytail.

Add a flash of fun with a sparkly design on your face, arm, ankle, or the back of your hand. Use a toothpick to dot corn syrup on your skin. Press on tiny flat-backed rhinestones or sequins. Let dry.

Buy a can of glitter hairspray—for anyone who wants a spritz of glitz!

Hang strings of white lights around the party room. Metallic streamers and helium balloons, available at party supply shops, will also add shine.

Paint fingernails with glittery nail polish.

Make napkin rings from star garland.

71

Shine On!

Use jewel glue to add rhinestones and craft jewels to sunglasses or picture frames—or both! Want something even cooler? Take a picture of everyone in sparkly shades. Include copies in your thank-you notes for girls to add to their sparkly frames. Everyone will have a glowing memory of the fun you had.

Sweet Sparklers

Stick frilly toothpicks into mini marshmallows. Dip each marshmallow into milk and then into Jell-O powder or Pop Rocks candy. To serve, arrange your sparkly treats on a foil tray or a glass plate lined with a foil doily.

Fun Fizz

In a punch bowl, mix any flavor of unsweetened drink powder with ½ cup sugar and 2 quarts cold water. Add a can of frozen grape juice concentrate and stir until dissolved. Pour in a 2-liter bottle of cold ginger ale and stir gently. Serve in Glittery Glasses.

Sparkly Spritzers

Mix fruit punch and lemon-lime soda in a pitcher or punch bowl. Add club soda for extra fizzzzzz! Serve in Glittery Glasses.

Glittery Glasses

Use glitter glue or fabric paint to write guests' names on plastic party glasses. Decorate with rhinestone stickers. Guests can rinse glasses after use and keep as favors.

Twinkle, Twinkle . . . You're a Star!

Each girl writes on a slip of paper a silly talent that she has. An example might be "I can sing the alphabet backward," or "I can put my foot behind my head." Put all the slips into a shoebox. Take turns drawing a slip from the box and trying to guess whose talent it is. If you're right, the girl performs her talent. But if you're wrong, you have to try to do it!

Videotape the silliness and watch your talented performances later.

"S-p-a-r-k-l-e" Game

Here's a fun twist on a school spelling game. Players stand in a circle. One girl starts spelling a word by saying a letter ("F"). Continuing around the circle, each girl says a letter. The object is to spell a real word.

For example, players' letters might be "F-R-I-E-N-D." The next player could stay in the game by adding "S." The next players might be able to think quickly enough to add "H-I-P" to spell "friendship." If you can't think of a letter to make a word, say "sparkle," and sit down. The last girl standing wins!

Glam Finale

Frost your favorite layer cake with white icing (or buy one already frosted). Sprinkle the cake with edible glittery cake sparkles. Top it off with fancy sparkler candles. Dim the lights when it's time to eat.

 Remember, only adults should light candles.

Sparkly Smile

Don't forget to go to sleep with sparkly teeth! Get a tube of "sparkle" toothpaste for everyone to try.

A Toast to the Host!

Drink sparkling grape juice cocktail in your Glittery Glasses and make star cutouts from toast with a star-shaped cookie cutter. Top toast with butter and jelly or cinnamon and sugar.

Glittery Gifts

There are lots of bright ideas for glittery party favors. From colorful glitter pencils, shiny stickers, glittery bouncy balls, tiny picture frames, to glitter hair accessories, body glitter, lip gloss, and sparkly temporary tattoos—your guests will love anything you can find that shines!

More Dream Themes

For your next sleepover, try one of these.

Dinner Party

Get fancy with your friends! Plan a nice meal, dress up, set the table, dim the lights, and dine!

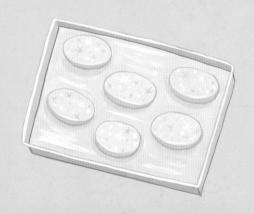

Eat-za Pizza Party!

Send takeout-menu-style invites. Start with make-your-own mini pizzas for dinner, followed by a yummy dessert pizza (see the one on page 39 of the Cocoa Loco Party). Wake up to—you guessed it— breakfast pizza!

Cookie Party

Mix up a double (or triple!) batch of sugar cookie dough. Divide girls into groups and have each group experiment with a different variation of mix-ins (from peanuts and marshmallows to raisins and M&M's). For fun, have each group create a commercial for its "famous" homemade cookies. After 15 minutes of practice, videotape the persuasive presentations. Watch them all later while you sample the goods with big bowls of cookies-and-cream or chocolate-chip-cookie-dough ice cream.

RED-HOT FIESTA SIESTA

Go to your library, get some salsa tunes, and start dancing! When everyone's hungry, dig in at a taco bar. Make crepe-paper flowers. For favors, give mini cacti, cinnamon candies, and red-hot nail polish!

Charity Bash

In place of gifts, ask guests to bring dog food for the Humane Society, toys for a local children's center, or canned goods for a food pantry. Activities might be to make crafts or baked goods to sell as a fund-raiser for the cause.

Party Animal

Pick your favorite pet, then build a theme. Try a Dog-Gone Fun Party if you like puppies, or a Cat's Pajamas Party if kittens are more your thing. Like them both? How about an It's Raining Cats and Dogs Party? The sky's the limit for food, craft, and activity ideas.

Share your slumber party ideas!
Send them to:

Snooze-a-Palooza Editor
American Girl
P.O. Box 620998
8400 Fairway Place
Middleton, WI 53562

Sorry, photos cannot be returned.

Here are some other American Girl books you might like:

❑ I read it.

❑ I read it.

❑ I read it.

❑ I read it.

❑ I read it.

❑ I read it.

Board Silly

Invitation
Matchboxes (1 per invite)
Checkered paper
Red & white paper
Red & black craft foam
Glue
White gel pen
Hole punch

Tic-Snack-Toe
Cupcakes
Frosting
Decorator icing
M&M's

You Don't Say!
Play money—from a game
    or homemade ($500 per guest)

Dice Cream
Half-gallon carton vanilla ice
    cream
Mini chocolate sandwich cookies

Games on the Go
Empty metal candy tins
    (1 per guest)
Acrylic paint
Paintbrushes
Magnetic sheets
Stickers
Scissors

(over)

Beadazzled Birthday

Invitation
Metal-rimmed key tags (1 per invite)
Candy bracelets (1 per invite)

Chill Out
Melon baller
Several pints ice cream
Plastic wrap

Twirl the Girl/Speed Bead
Beads (different colors)

Bead-Happy Bracelets
Wide embroidered ribbon
Fabric glue
24-gauge craft wire (2 feet per guest)
Seed beads
Buttons with shank (1 per guest)
Scissors
Ruler
Fingernail clippers

Power Cookies
Fortune cookies
Chocolate chips
Candy sprinkles
Wax paper
Paper, pen, scissors
Hole punch
Beads
Thread

(over)

Monkey Business

Invitation
Scrapbook paper
Craft-foam shapes
Google eyes (2 per invite)
Paper fasteners (1 per invite)

Funky Monkey Milk Shakes
Chocolate ice cream
Milk
Peanut butter cups
Bananas
Whipped cream
Plastic monkeys (for decoration)

Monkey Tails
Bananas (1 per 2 guests)
Wooden sticks (1 per guest)
Wax paper
Toppings (chopped peanuts,
    colored sprinkles)
Chocolate sauce

Sock Monkeys
Red-Heel socks (1 pair per 2 guests)
Rubber bands
Small dried beans
Craft glue
Buttons (2 per guest)

(over)

Cupcake Faces
Chocolate frosting
Vanilla frosting
Cupcakes
Mini vanilla wafers
Mini peanut butter sandwich
  cookies
Red licorice whips
Mini M&M's

Miscellaneous
Rent movie *(Summer of the
Monkeys or Most Valuable Primate)*

Monkey Muffins
Chopped pecans
Cinnamon, sugar, brown sugar
Ziplock bags
Refrigerated buttermilk biscuits
Butter

Favors
Party bags (1 per guest)

Monkey-themed headbands •
bookmarks • pens • socks •
earrings

Beads & Charms
Cantaloupe (1 melon per 2 guests)
Blueberries
Grapes
Yogurt
Cereal

Favor Fun
Plastic bags (1 per guest)
Beads
Ribbon
Elastic cord (10-inch length per guest)

Fuzzy Dice
Fake fur cut into squares
Craft glue
Small wooden cubes (2 per guest)
Colorful rhinestones

Speed Games
Board games
Timer

Giant Goofball Game
Colored paper (3 sheets per guest)
Markers (1 per guest)
White paper
1 large square box
Black marker

Rise and Dine!
Frozen waffles

Peanut butter • jelly •
cream cheese • chocolate chips •
frozen yogurt • fruit

Key Chain Keepsakes
Key chain games (1 per guest)

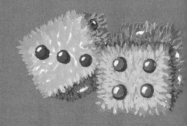

Cocoa loco

Invitation
Chocolate bars (1 per invite)
Scrapbook paper, pen, scissors
Stickers, tape

What's in Hot Chocolate?
Chocolate Hugs or Kisses

Special Delivery
Mini marshmallows
Butter or margarine
Chocolate chips
White chocolate chips
Chocolate crisp rice cereal
Maraschino cherries
Gummy worms

The Chocolate Game
Chocolate bar
Gift wrap
Ribbon
Small paper plates
Hat, scarf, gloves
Table knife and fork
2 dice

S'more Nachos
Flour tortillas
Creamy peanut butter
Mini chocolate chips
Mini marshmallows
Cooking spray

(over)

Brrr! day Party

Invitation
Paper
Fleece or felt
String

Ice Breaker
Stuffed animals

S'Mittens
Mittens or gloves (1 pair per guest)
Variety of ribbon trims, fake fur
Fabric glue

Snowballs
Crackers
Creamy peanut butter
White chocolate
Wax paper
M&M's

Cool Scarf
6-by-40-inch strips fleece (2 per guest)
Craft or fabric glue
Scissors for each guest (or to share)

Chilly Cheese Dip
Processed cheese
No-bean chili
Tortilla chips

Hot & Zesties
Mini smoked sausages
Barbecue sauce
Toothpicks or skewers

(over)

Scrapbook Bonanza

Invitation
Envelopes (1 per invite)
Scrapbook paper
Stickers

Paper Punch Confetti
Scrapbook paper
Variety of hole punches

Photo Cake
Photo or scrapbook page
Bakery cake
Fruit Roll-Ups
Confetti candy sprinkles

Scrapbook Supplies
Mini scrapbooks (1 per guest)
Alphabet stickers
Scrapbook paper (lots!)
Specialty scissors (to share)
Die cuts, photo frames, gel pens,
    markers
Photo corners
Double-sided tape (acid-free)

Table Talkers
Scrap paper
Pens

(over)

Scrap Bookmark
Extra scrapbook supplies (above)
Hole punch
Contact paper
Ribbon

Say "Cheese!"
(pick some)
Cheese puffs • cheese popcorn •
cheddar-flavored crackers •
cheese pizza • macaroni and
cheese • grilled cheese •
cheeseburgers

Confetti Cookies
Colored vanilla wafers
Frosting
Candy sequins or sprinkles

Confetti Eggs
Eggs
Red, yellow, and green peppers
Shredded cheddar or
    Monterey Jack cheese

Scrap Bags
Bags (1 per guest)
Disposable cameras (1 per guest)
Stickers
Scrapbook paper
Paper punches
Rubber stamps and ink pads
Gel pens
Photo corners
Paper die cuts

Stir It Up!
Plastic spoons
Dippers: white chocolate chips •
milk chocolate chips • butter-
scotch chips • peanut butter chips
• semisweet chocolate chips
Toppers: marshmallows • ice-
cream sprinkles • M&M's • cookies
• candies
Wax paper
Cellophane candy bags
Ribbon

Miscellaneous
Frosty nail polish

Rent movie (*Ice Age • Snow Dogs •
    Snow Day • Johnny Tsunami*)

Morning Frost
Frosted or powdered-sugar
    doughnuts
Juice

Cool Stuff
Cocoa mugs (1 per guest)
Minty gum
Ice cream gift certificates
Lip balm or gloss
Nail polish
Hot cocoa packet

Terrific Truffles
Semisweet chocolate chips
Sweetened condensed milk
Candy decorations
Paper candy cups
Small boxes (1 per guest)

Chocolate Chippers
Semisweet chocolate chips
Vanilla
Sugar
Pancake batter or mix
Maraschino cherries
Whipped cream
Chocolate milk

Miscellaneous
Rent movie (*Willy Wonka and the
    Chocolate Factory*)

Flavor-ite Favors
Bags (1 per guest)
Chocolate-scented soap, lotion,
    markers, or stickers
Chocolate-flavored lip gloss
Chocolate-themed earrings,
    hairbows, or magnets

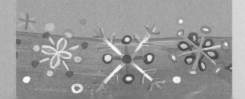

Glitter Gala

Invitation
Crepe-paper streamer, paper, pen
Star garland

You Glow, Girl!
Body glitter
Metallic star garland/pipe cleaners
Glitter hairspray
Strings of white lights
Metallic streamers
Toothpicks
Corn syrup
Flat-backed rhinestones or
    sequins
Glittery nail polish
Star garland
Helium balloons

Shine On!
Sunglasses and/or plain picture
    frames (1 per guest)
Flat-backed rhinestones or craft
    jewels
Jewel glue

Sweet Sparklers
Frilly toothpicks
Mini marshmallows
Jell-O powder
Pop Rocks candy
Milk
Foil tray and/or foil doily

(over)

Spa Night!

Invitation
Construction paper
Glue
Marabou
Fuzzy pipe cleaners
Pom-poms

Spa Berries
Strawberries
White or milk chocolate
Wax paper

Powder Puffs
Frozen puff pastry shells
Whipped topping
Powdered sugar

Cool Cucumbers
Cucumbers
Cream cheese
Dry ranch dressing mix
Sour cream
Mini bagels
Fresh dill sprig

(over)

Spa Night!

Relaxation Station
Handheld massage rollers
    (1 per guest)

Lotion Sampler
Lotions (different types)

Paste Test
Fun-flavored toothpastes

Smart Start
Frozen fruit (strawberries,
    blueberries, bananas)
Orange juice
Yogurt (1 container per batch)

Miscellaneous
Rent a yoga video

Pamper Packs
Washcloths
Travel-sized shampoos
Travel-sized lotions
Nail clippers
Combs
Hairbrushes
Nailbrushes
Ribbons

Head-to-Toe Treatment

Face

Bananas
Honey
Cornmeal
Cucumbers
Washcloths (1 per guest)
Ponytail holders or headbands

Hands

Sugar
Baby oil
Nail polish remover (tub kind)
Lemon juice
Milk
Olive oil
Nail polish

American Curls

Fabric strips
Spray bottle

Spa Supplies

Cotton balls	Mini shampoos
Cotton swabs	Mini lotions
Washcloths	Nail clippers
Ponytail holders	Nail polishes
Mini soaps	Hairbrushes
Lip gloss tubes	Combs
Toothbrushes	Hair clips
Nailbrushes	

Fun Fizz

Unsweetened drink powder
Sugar
Frozen grape juice concentrate
Ginger ale

Sparkly Spritzers

Fruit punch
Lemon-lime soda
Club soda (optional)

Glittery Glasses

Plastic party glasses (1 per guest)
Glitter glue or fabric paint
Rhinestone stickers

Glam Finale

Layer cake or cake mix
and frosting
Glittery cake sparkles
Sparkler candles

Sparkly Smile

"Sparkle" toothpaste

A Toast to the Host!

Sparkling grape juice cocktail
Bread
Star-shaped cookie cutter
Butter or margarine
Jelly or cinnamon and sugar

Glittery Gifts

Plastic bags (1 per guest)

Glittery pencils • stickers • bouncy
balls • picture frames • hair accessories • lip gloss • body glitter •
temporary tattoos

(continued)